MW00882941

Bitcoin for the Working Class

A Blue-Collar Guide to Financial Freedom

"A government big enough to give you eveything you want, is a government big enough to take from you everything you have."

-Gerald R. Ford,
38th President of the United States

Bitcoin for the Working Class

A Blue-Collar Guide to Financial Freedom

Captain Matt Jackson

Copyright © 2024 by "Captain Matt Jackson"

All rights reserved. This book or any portion thereof may not be reproduced or used in any manner whatsoever without the express written permission of the publisher, except for the use of brief quotations in a book review.

Disclaimer

The information provided in "Bitcoin for the Working Class: A Blue-Collar Guide to Financial Freedom" is for general informational purposes only. All information in the book is provided in good faith, however, we make no representation or warranty of any kind, express or implied, regarding the accuracy, adequacy, validity, reliability, availability, or completeness of any information in the book.

The author is not a financial advisor, nor does he provide personalized financial advice. The contents of this book are not intended to be a substitute for professional financial advice. Always seek the advice of a qualified financial advisor with any questions you may have regarding a financial matter.

Any action you take upon the information in this book is strictly at your own risk, and the author will not be liable for any losses or damages in connection with the use of our book. The readers are encouraged to think critically and consult professional advice before making any financial decisions.

This book does not promote or endorse any specific investment strategy, and it does not guarantee the performance or success of any investment. Cryptocurrency investments are inherently volatile and risky, and readers are advised to conduct their own research and due diligence.

By using this book, you agree to the above disclaimer and acknowledge that the author and publisher are not liable for any financial losses or other damages caused directly or indirectly by the content of this book.

Dedication

To the working class—the true backbone of this country,

This book is dedicated to you, the unsung heroes who build, maintain, and energize the veins of our nation. You clock in every day, giving your sweat and grit to tasks that keep the wheels of progress turning. You're not just working hard; you're crafting the framework of our future.

You are the foundation upon which this great land stands, and you deserve every ounce of success you've earned, plus a little extra for your smarts and unwavering spirit. May this guide serve as a tool of inspiration in your hands, one that helps you carve a path to financial freedom and prosperity.

Here's to building a future where your efforts are met with the wealth you've rightly earned—may you find clarity in these pages and confidence in your actions as you navigate the new terrain of Bitcoin and digital currency.

With respect and admiration,

Captain Matt Jackson

Contents

Foreward

Get ready, because you're about to break into the world of Bitcoin, and it's not for the faint of heart. "Bitcoin for the Working Class: A Blue-Collar Guide to Financial Freedom" is more than just a manual—it's your entry ticket to the financial revolution that's been taking the elite by storm, now made accessible for the everyday man.

As someone who has been in the financial trenches, I've seen shiny new things come and go, but Bitcoin is a different beast. It's tough, resilient, and it's changing the game. This isn't some overblown tech wizardry or Wall Street jargon; this is real, hard-hitting, practical know-how, served up by a fire captain who knows what it means to handle the heat.

Bitcoin isn't just another currency; it's a shot at real freedom. It's about taking the power back from oversized banks and putting it right where it belongs—your hands. It's about not just earning your pay, but making it work for you on a global scale, no middlemen, no BS.

This book is your no-nonsense guide to everything Bitcoin. From cracking the code on what Bitcoin really is, to tactical advice on how I was able to buy, store, and grow my Bitcoin stash, it's all here. You'll get the straight scoop, the tools, and the savvy to navigate the risks and reap the rewards.

Whether you're throwing down your first Satoshi or looking to beef up your investment strategy, let this guide light your path. You're not just reading up on an investment; you're gearing up for battle in the financial wilds.

Get ready to arm yourself with knowledge and charge into the fray. The world of Bitcoin waits for no one, and with this book in hand, you're set to take it by storm.

Captain Matt Jackson

Introduction:

Dive Into the Bitcoin Revolution

Welcome to the no-nonsense world of Bitcoin, where the pace is fast and the potential is huge. Before you dive into the pages ahead, let's strap on our gear and lay the groundwork for this no BS guide through the universe of digital gold. And who better to guide you than a seasoned fire captain? That's right, this isn't just any finance guide—it's written from the perspective of someone who knows all about managing heat, handling pressure, and making quick, decisive moves.

Why a fire captain? Because in both firefighting and Bitcoin, you need a cool head, a clear plan, and the guts to see it through when things get tough. This guide is your trusty companion, ready to roll through the mud and grit of Bitcoin, crafted by someone who's no stranger to hard work, and navigating chaos with expertise and authority.

Why Bitcoin? Because it's changing the finance game the way power tools changed construction—making things faster, more efficient, and a heck of a lot more powerful.

It's immediate, it spans the globe, and it cuts through the red tape like a hot knife through butter. But there's more to Bitcoin than just a chance to make a quick buck—it's about taking control, joining a community, and being part of one of the biggest shifts in money management we've ever seen.

In this book, we'll break down the what, why, and how of Bitcoin—consider this your basic training. We'll tackle how to safely buy and store Bitcoin, steer clear of pitfalls, and protect your hard-earned cash. We'll take you through Bitcoin's highs and lows, explore the nuts and bolts that keep it running, and pull up a chair to the table where the big debates are happening.

Throughout the book you may notice certain facts and concepts appear more than once. This repetition is by design, strategically implemented to reinforce key points and ensure they stick with you. Remembering these essential insights is crucial as you navigate the world of Bitcoin and make informed decisions about your financial future.

And because nobody learns just by going it alone, we'll show you how to connect with other folks in the Bitcoin scene, keep your knowledge fresh, and play it smart and secure in the crypto world.

So, lace up your boots and let's get moving. This book isn't just about reading—it's about doing. It's time to jump into the action and see what Bitcoin can do for you. Let's get our hands dirty and dive headfirst into the Bitcoin revolution.

Chapter 1:

What is Bitcoin?

Introduction to Money

Alright, crew, gather 'round! Let's talk about something that's shaking things up in the world of money. Now, we all know what money is, right? It's those bills in your wallet, the coins in your pocket, the numbers on your bank statement. But where did it all start? Picture this: way back when, people didn't have money. That's right, they traded stuff. Got a goat? Need some grain? You'd have to find someone who wanted your goat and had grain to trade. Could you imagine if we were still doing that today? It's like trying to find a fire hydrant in the desert—frustrating and slow.

Then, some genius came up with the idea of coins. Suddenly, you didn't need to carry your goat everywhere. Coins were lighter and easier to trade. Fast forward a few centuries, and now we've got paper money, credit cards, and all that jazz. But here's the kicker—money's evolving again, and this time, it's going digital. Enter Bitcoin.

What is Bitcoin?

So, what's this Bitcoin thing I'm talking about? Think of it like this: Bitcoin is money for the internet. But it's not the kind of money you can stuff under your mattress or lose in the couch cushions. It's digital, which means it only exists online. No coins, no bills—just numbers on a screen. But don't let that fool you; Bitcoin's as real as the smoke you see during a fire. You might not be able to touch it, but you can sure as heck see its impact and spend it.

Now, here's where it gets interesting: no one's in charge of Bitcoin. No government, no bank, no CEO. It's like a well-trained firefighting team that doesn't need a boss to get things done. Bitcoin works because everyone involved plays by the same rules, and those rules are set in stone—or, more accurately, in code.

This system keeps everything above board and prevents any funny business, like double-spending or counterfeiting. This built in accounting system actually keeps better track of transactions than the bean counters for the federal government!

Why Bitcoin is Different

So, why should you care about Bitcoin? Let me tell you why. Traditional money—dollars, euros, whatever—can be printed by governments whenever they feel like it. And when they print too much, it's like throwing gasoline on a fire: you get inflation. Your money loses value, and before you know it, that dollar in your pocket isn't worth squat. At the time of this writing, August 2024, the dollar has depreciated around 20% since 2020, this is due to outrageous government spending. Most of us blue-collar workers' paychecks are not keeping up with this level of inflation through COLA's (cost of living adjustments) which is driving us to find second jobs or higher paying opportunities.

But Bitcoin? Bitcoin's got a built-in limit. <u>There will _only_ ever be 21 million Bitcoins</u>, period. No one can make more, which means it's immune to inflation.

It's like having a water supply that never runs dry during a fire—always reliable, always valuable.

And here's another thing: Bitcoin doesn't care about borders. You can send it to anyone, anywhere, anytime. No banks, little to no fees, no waiting. It's like driving a fire truck straight through traffic because nothing's going to stop you from reaching your destination.

Bitcoin's different because it puts you in control. It's your money, your rules. No one can freeze it, seize it, or tell you how to spend it. It's financial freedom in your back pocket.

That's the basics, folks. Bitcoin is the future of money, and it's not waiting for anyone to catch up. Whether you're ready or not, it's here, and it's blazing a trail in the financial world. Next up, we're diving into where this digital dynamo came from, and why it's got everyone from Wall Street to Main Street talking. Stay tuned, and stay on your toes, we're just getting started.

Chapter 2:

The Birth of Bitcoin

The Story of Bitcoin

Alright, team, let's rewind the clock to the mysterious birth of Bitcoin. This tale begins in 2008, right in the middle of a global financial meltdown. Banks were crumbling, people were losing their savings, and trust in the system was about as solid as a house of cards. Enter Satoshi Nakamoto, a person (or maybe a group—no one really knows) who decided enough was enough. Satoshi had a vision: a new kind of money that didn't rely on banks, governments, or any middlemen. And just like that, the idea of Bitcoin was born.

Satoshi wrote a whitepaper—a sort of blueprint— explaining how Bitcoin would work. This wasn't some pie-in-the-sky dream.

This was a plan to create digital money that was secure, decentralized, and limited in supply. The title of the whitepaper? "Bitcoin: A Peer-to-Peer Electronic Cash System." Catchy, huh? It laid out the foundation for a currency that anyone could use, anywhere, without needing to trust anyone but the code itself.

Then, in January 2009, Satoshi released the first version of Bitcoin's software, and the first-ever block of Bitcoin —called the "genesis block"—was mined. This was the moment Bitcoin came to life, quietly and without fanfare, like the first crack of dawn before a wildfire spreads.

The First Bitcoin Transaction

Now, let me tell you about the first big moment in Bitcoin history, a story that's become legendary. It's May 22, 2010. A guy named Laszlo Hanyecz in Florida decides he's hungry. But instead of paying for pizza with cash or a credit card, he offered to pay with Bitcoin. At the time, Bitcoin was worth next to nothing —just some digital curiosity with a few cents of value. Laszlo convinced someone to accept 10,000 Bitcoins in exchange for two pizzas. That's right, 10,000 Bitcoins for a couple of pies.

Today, those Bitcoins would be worth hundreds of millions of dollars. But back then? Just two pizzas.

This wasn't just a meal. It was a proof of concept: Bitcoin could be used as real money, for real things. It was like the first time someone tried using a fire hose and realized, "Hey, this thing actually works!"

Bitcoin's Growth

After that first bite of pizza, Bitcoin didn't just sit around. It started growing, and fast.

At first, it was mostly tech geeks, cryptographers, and a few rebels who saw the potential. But as more people got involved, Bitcoin's value started to rise. Slowly at first, then like a freight train.

By 2011, Bitcoin hit parity with the US dollar— 1 Bitcoin equaled 1 dollar. Not long after, it kept climbing. People were starting to notice. Media outlets began running stories, and Bitcoin exchanges popped up, making it easier for people to buy and sell this digital currency. Bitcoin was no longer just an experiment; it was becoming a force to be reckoned with.

Why People Believe in Bitcoin

So, why did Bitcoin catch on? Why did people start believing in this digital currency that seemed like something out of a sci-fi movie? It boils down to a few key things.

First, Bitcoin is different from anything that had come before. It is decentralized—no central bank, no government, no single point of failure. It was like a fire truck that didn't need a driver—just a team working together, each one doing their part. And because it is decentralized, <u>Bitcoin is seen as resistant to censorship and control.</u> No one could stop you from sending or receiving it.

Second, Bitcoin is scarce. There will only ever be 21 million Bitcoins, which means it can't be inflated away like paper money. People started calling it "digital gold" because, like gold, it is seen as a store of value—a way to protect your wealth from the fires of inflation.

Lastly, Bitcoin is global. It doesn't care where you live, what language you speak, or which currency you use. You could send Bitcoin across the world as easily as sending an email. It is money for the internet age, and that's what makes it powerful.

That's the origin story of Bitcoin, straight out of the ashes of a broken financial system. It was born from frustration, built by visionaries, and fueled by a belief in something better.

In the next chapter, we'll dive into the nitty-gritty of how Bitcoin is created, through a process called mining. It's time to roll up our sleeves and see what's happening behind the scenes. Stay sharp!

Chapter 3:

Bitcoin Mining

What is Bitcoin Mining?

Alright, crew, it's time to roll up our sleeves and dig into one of the most crucial parts of the Bitcoin world: mining. Now, I know what you're thinking—"Mining? Like digging for gold?" Well, sort of, but without the pickaxes and dirt. Let's break it down.

Bitcoin mining is the process of creating new Bitcoins and keeping the Bitcoin network secure. Imagine a big digital ledger that keeps track of all Bitcoin transactions. This ledger is called the blockchain, and every time someone sends or receives Bitcoin, it gets recorded in this ledger. But here's the catch: before a new transaction can be added to the blockchain, it needs to be verified. That's where miners come in.

Miners use powerful computers to solve complex mathematical puzzles. When a miner solves one of these puzzles, they get to add a new block of transactions to the blockchain.

Think of it like a race—whichever miner solves the puzzle first gets to add the block and earns a reward in the form of new Bitcoin. This reward is like the prize money in a race, and it's the only way new Bitcoin is created. Without miners, there'd be no new Bitcoin and no one to keep the network secure.

The Energy Question

Now, let's address the elephant in the room—energy use. You might have heard that Bitcoin mining uses a lot of electricity, and you'd be right. All those powerful computers working day and night to solve puzzles don't come cheap in terms of energy. Critics argue that this energy use is wasteful and harmful to the environment. But let's dig a little deeper before jumping to conclusions.

Yes, Bitcoin mining does use a lot of energy, but so do many other industries.

The real question is whether that energy use is justified and how it compares to other financial systems. Think about all the energy used by banks, ATMs, and data centers around the world. The traditional financial system is no energy lightweight either. And unlike traditional finance, Bitcoin is a decentralized network that provides financial services without needing massive office buildings, armies of staff, or endless paperwork.

Just look at how many credit card offers you receive in the mail every day. Where are the upset tree huggers with all that wasteful printing? Because those offers usually go straight in the trash and yet, no one is raising hell over that annoying bullsh*t.

But that's not to say Bitcoin mining can't improve.

It can, and it is. Which brings us to our next point: green energy. So if you're one of those tree huggers out there, make sure you pay close attention, as I'm sure the loons in the mainstream media and government already poisoned your brain! There is still hope, so just go into this with an open mind.

Green Energy and Mining

Here's where things get interesting. While it's true that Bitcoin mining uses a lot of energy, there's a growing trend towards using renewable energy sources. Miners are starting to realize that going green isn't just good for the planet—it's good for business too.

Renewable energy sources like solar, wind, and hydroelectric power are becoming more popular among Bitcoin miners. Why? Because they're often cheaper in the long run. Once the infrastructure is in place, the cost of producing energy from renewable sources is much lower than using fossil fuels. Plus, some miners are setting up shop in places where renewable energy is abundant and underutilized, like in certain parts of Iceland or the Pacific Northwest, where geothermal and hydroelectric power are plentiful.

In fact, some mining operations are already powered almost entirely by renewable energy. Take **Genesis Mining** in Iceland, for example. Their mining farms are powered by 100% renewable energy, thanks to the country's abundant geothermal and hydroelectric resources. And they're not alone—more and more miners are making the switch to green energy as they recognize the long-term benefits.

Another cool innovation is miners using energy that would otherwise go to waste. In places like Texas, some miners are tapping into natural gas that's being flared off from oil production. Instead of letting that gas go up in smoke, they're using it to power their mining rigs. It's a win-win: reducing waste and generating Bitcoin at the same time.

Why Mining is Important

So, why does all this mining matter? Why should we care about these miners and their energy use? Here's the deal: miners are the lifeblood of the Bitcoin network. Without them, there would be no new Bitcoins, and the entire system would grind to a halt.

Miners play a critical role in securing the Bitcoin network. Every time a miner adds a new block of transactions to the blockchain, they're helping to protect the network from fraud and attacks. The more miners there are, the harder it is for anyone to mess with the system. It's like having a whole crew of firefighters on call, ready to respond to any emergency. The more hands on deck, the safer everyone is.

Mining also keeps the Bitcoin supply in check. Remember that reward miners get for adding a new block? That's how new Bitcoin is created, but it doesn't happen all at once. The reward gets smaller over time, which means fewer new Bitcoins are being created as time goes on. This gradual reduction in supply is built into the system and helps to ensure that Bitcoin remains valuable over the long haul.

In a nutshell, Bitcoin mining is about much more than just creating new coins. It's about keeping the network secure, decentralized, and running smoothly. And as the industry continues to evolve, we're seeing more innovation and a growing focus on sustainability. Bitcoin is here to stay, and mining is the engine that keeps it all running.

Alright, team, that's the scoop on Bitcoin mining. It's not just about making new coins—it's about securing the network, embracing green energy, and ensuring the future of digital money. As we roll into the next chapter, we'll see how Bitcoin has made its mark in the real world, from countries adopting it, to companies accepting it. So stay sharp - this fire is just getting started!

Chapter 4:

Bitcoin in the Real World

Countries Using Bitcoin

Alright, folks, let's take a look at how Bitcoin is blazing trails across the globe. You might think Bitcoin is just a fancy tech experiment or something only used by people who are allergic to banks. But the truth is, Bitcoin is making waves in the real world, especially in countries where the financial system is on shaky ground.

First up, El Salvador. In 2021, this small Central American country did something bold—it became the first country in the world to adopt Bitcoin as legal tender. That's right, folks. In El Salvador, you can walk into a store and buy your morning coffee with Bitcoin. The government even launched an app called "Chivo Wallet" to make it easy for people to use.

Why did they do this? Simple: the country wanted to give people an alternative to the US dollar, which was their official currency. They saw Bitcoin as a way to attract investment, boost the economy, and help people who don't have access to traditional banks.

But it's not just El Salvador. Other countries are watching closely and some are even dipping their toes in the water. In places like Nigeria, Argentina, and Venezuela, where inflation is running wild and trust in the local currency is low, people are turning to Bitcoin as a safe haven for their money. It's like finding a fireproof safe in the middle of a blaze—people are looking for something that won't burn up with the rest of their savings.

Bitcoin in Business

Now, let's talk business. You might be surprised to learn that some pretty big names are getting in on the Bitcoin action. We're talking about companies that have announced they've added Bitcoin to their balance sheets, making it part of their investment portfolios. These aren't just fly-by-night operations—these are serious, established businesses that see the potential in Bitcoin.

Let's start with **MicroStrategy**, the business intelligence firm led by CEO Michael Saylor. They were one of the first major companies to go all-in on Bitcoin, buying up over 100,000 Bitcoins since 2020. Saylor has been one of Bitcoin's most vocal advocates, calling it "digital gold" and urging other companies to follow suit. As of now, MicroStrategy holds more Bitcoin than any other publicly traded company.

Next up, **Tesla**, the electric car giant led by Elon Musk. In early 2021, Tesla made headlines by purchasing $1.5 billion worth of Bitcoin, and for a while, they even accepted Bitcoin as payment for their cars.

Although they paused the Bitcoin payment option due to concerns about the environmental impact of Bitcoin mining, Tesla's move was a major milestone in Bitcoin's journey toward mainstream acceptance.

Then there's **Square** (now known as Block), the payment processing company founded by Twitter co-founder Jack Dorsey. Square bought $50 million worth of Bitcoin in October 2020 and added another $170 million in February 2021. Dorsey has been a long-time supporter of Bitcoin, seeing it as the future of the internet and even funding development projects to improve the Bitcoin ecosystem.

Galaxy Digital, the cryptocurrency investment firm founded by former hedge fund manager Mike Novogratz, is another big player. Galaxy Digital has a substantial Bitcoin position as part of its broader cryptocurrency investment strategy, making it one of the largest institutional holders of Bitcoin.

We also have **Coinbase**, one of the world's largest cryptocurrency exchanges, which added Bitcoin to its balance sheet in 2021. Coinbase's move was a natural fit, given that their entire business revolves around cryptocurrency, but it still sent a strong message about the long-term viability of Bitcoin as an investment.

Other companies like **Marathon Digital Holdings, Riot Blockchain, and Hut 8 Mining Corp**, —all major players in the Bitcoin mining industry—also hold substantial amounts of Bitcoin as part of their investment strategies. These companies are betting big on the future of Bitcoin, both as a currency and as an asset.

These companies represent just the tip of the iceberg. Every day, more businesses are exploring how they can incorporate Bitcoin into their operations, whether as an investment, a payment method, or even as part of their treasury management strategies.

It's clear that Bitcoin isn't just a fringe idea anymore—
it's becoming a central part of the financial landscape.

Bitcoin for the Unbanked

Here's where things get really interesting. In many parts
of the world, millions of people don't have access to a
bank. They can't get a loan, they can't save their money
safely, and they can't send or receive money without
paying sky-high fees. **Enter Bitcoin.**

In places like Africa, Southeast Asia, and Latin
America, Bitcoin is giving people a way to participate in
the global economy. All you need is a smartphone and
an internet connection, and you can start using Bitcoin.
This is a game-changer for people who've been left out
of the traditional financial system. It's like handing
someone a fire extinguisher when they've never had one
before—they finally have a tool to protect themselves
from that inferno called inflation.

Take, for example, Nigeria. The country has a young,
tech-savvy population, but many people don't have
access to traditional banking. Bitcoin has become a
popular way to save, invest, and do business.

It's the same story in Venezuela, where hyperinflation has made the local currency almost worthless. People are turning to Bitcoin to preserve their wealth and keep their heads above water.

Challenges Bitcoin Faces

Now, let's not sugarcoat it—Bitcoin's got its challenges. First off, there's the volatility. Bitcoin's price can swing wildly, sometimes gaining or losing thousands of dollars in a single day. That kind of instability can be a tough pill to swallow, especially if you're relying on it for everyday transactions. It's like trying to drive a fire truck on a rollercoaster—not exactly smooth sailing.

Then there's the regulatory landscape. Governments around the world are still figuring out how to handle Bitcoin. Some countries, like China, have cracked down hard, banning Bitcoin mining and trading. Others, like the US, are trying to find a balance between fostering innovation and protecting consumers. The truth is, no one really knows where the regulation hammer is going to fall, and that uncertainty can be a big risk.

And let's not forget public perception. Despite all the success stories, some people still see Bitcoin as shady, risky, or just plain confusing. There's a learning curve, and not everyone is willing to climb it. That's why I believe it's our job to help spread the word and clear up the misconceptions—because the more people understand Bitcoin, the stronger it becomes.

So there you have it, the real-world impact of Bitcoin. It's not just some digital fantasy—it's a powerful tool that's being used by countries, businesses, and everyday people around the globe. But like any tool, it's got its pros and cons, and it's up to each of us to figure out how to wield it. On to the next chapter—grab your gear, and let's keep moving!

Chapter 5:

The Road to Financial Freedom

How Bitcoin Can Create Financial Freedom

Alright, buckle up! Let's talk about something every man loves: freedom. Financial freedom, that is. Bitcoin isn't just digital cash—it's a chance to break free from the old chains of banks and bulky wallets. Here's how Bitcoin is lighting up the path to financial freedom;

No Inflation: Unlike traditional money, which can be printed on a government's whim, Bitcoin has a cap. That's right—only 21 million Bitcoins will ever exist. This limit is coded right into the system, making Bitcoin immune to inflation. It's like having a fireproof safe for your money; no matter how much heat the economy takes, your Bitcoin keeps its value. Whether you own 1 Bitcoin or 1% of a Bitcoin you own that amount of Bitcoin and no one can take that from you!

Protection Against Corrupt Governments: Bitcoin doesn't care about borders or bureaucrats. It operates on a global network that's out of reach from overly handsy governments. For people living under unstable regimes where money can be seized or savings can vanish with a change in policy, Bitcoin is like an escape ladder in a smoke-filled building—always there, ready to help you get out.

Success Stories

Now, who doesn't love a good success story? Since Bitcoin hit the scene, there have been plenty of rags-to-riches tales that make even the lottery look like a bad bet.

Take the story of Erik Finman, for instance. This guy bought Bitcoin at the age of 12 with $1,000 from his grandmother. By the time he was 18, he was a millionaire. Or how about that Norwegian man who bought $27 worth of Bitcoin in 2009, forgot about it, and found out it was worth over $850,000 in 2013? These stories aren't just urban legends; they're real-life examples of how Bitcoin has changed lives.

And it's not just individuals—entire companies have been built on Bitcoin investments. Companies that got in early on Bitcoin have seen their fortunes soar as the value of Bitcoin rocketed from pennies to thousands of dollars.

Risks to Consider

But hold your horses—before you jump all in, let's talk risks. Bitcoin, like any good adventure, has its share of dragons to slay:

Volatility: Bitcoin's price can be as unpredictable as a backdraft. One minute it's calm, the next it's blowing the roof off. This kind of volatility can mean big gains, but also big losses, so it's not for the faint of heart.

Security Risks: While Bitcoin itself is secure, the places where you buy, sell, and store it might not be. Exchanges can be hacked, wallets can be lost, and if you're not careful, your Bitcoin can vanish faster than a drop of water on a hot skillet.

Regulatory Risks: Bitcoin operates in a legal gray area in many parts of the world. New regulations can affect its value and use, so keeping an eye on the news is crucial. The world however, is becoming more accepting as of lately.

How to Safely Invest

Ready to take the plunge?
Here's how to do it without getting burned:

Do Your Homework: Understand what you're getting into. Read up, talk to experienced Bitcoin users, and get a solid grasp of how it all works.

Start Small: Don't put all your eggs in one basket, especially when that basket is as bouncy as Bitcoin. Start with small amounts, get the hang of it, and just like any investment, only invest what you can afford to lose. DCA (Dollar Cost Average) into a position buying small chunks over an extended period of time no matter the price of Bitcoin.

Use Reputable Exchanges: Stick to well-known, well-regarded exchanges for buying and selling Bitcoin. And once you've bought your Bitcoin, move it into a secure wallet—preferably a hardware wallet that keeps your Bitcoin offline and out of reach from hackers.

Keep Your Private Keys Private: Your private key is what keeps your Bitcoin yours. If someone gets it, they can swipe your Bitcoin quicker than the tax man stealing your paycheck. Keep it secret, keep it safe.

Stay Informed: The world of Bitcoin moves fast. Keep an eye on developments, both technological and regulatory, to make smart, informed decisions.

That's the road to financial freedom, folks. Bitcoin offers a new way to think about money, one that puts the power back in your hands. But remember, with great power comes great responsibility. Be smart, be safe, and who knows? Maybe you'll be the next Bitcoin success story in your group of friends that everyone is talking about. Next up, we'll explore how to get in on the Bitcoin action yourself—whether you want to invest, save, or just stay ahead of the curve. Stay tuned, and stay sharp!

Chapter 6:

How to Invest in Bitcoin

Getting Started with Bitcoin

Alright, team, let's gear up and dive into the Bitcoin investment world. First thing's first: buying Bitcoin. You're not gonna find this digital gold lying around on the sidewalk. You've gotta know where to shop.

Using Exchanges: Think of Bitcoin exchanges like the firehouses of the Bitcoin world. They're the go-to spots to get your hands on some Bitcoin. Platforms like **Coinbase, Binance, and Kraken** are like the big, bustling fire stations—they've got all the tools and gadgets. You create an account, verify your identity (gotta keep things above board), and link a payment method like a bank account or credit card.

Then, just like buying anything online, you put in an order for how much Bitcoin you want, and boom—you're in business.

Peer-to-Peer (P2P) Platforms: Want to skip the middleman? P2P platforms like **Paxful** let you buy directly from other people. It's like having a direct line to another firefighter instead of going through dispatch. Just be extra cautious—deal only with users who have stellar reputations to avoid getting scammed.

Storing Your Bitcoin Safely

Once you've got your Bitcoin, you need to keep it safe. Bitcoin wallets are the equivalent of a lock on your front door—without a good one, you're in trouble.

Hot Wallets: These are online wallets, handy for quick access and daily use, but they're also more vulnerable to hacks. It's like keeping your wallet on the table next to the front door—quick to grab but risky if someone breaks in.

Cold Wallets: These are offline wallets, much more secure. They're like storing your most valuable items in a locked, fireproof safe. Hardware wallets like **Ledger** or **Trezor** are popular choices—they store your Bitcoin on a physical device that only connects to the internet when you need it to.

Security Practices: Always use strong, unique passwords for your accounts and wallets. Enable two-factor authentication (2FA) everywhere you can. This is like double-locking your front door. And **backup your wallet's recovery phrases securely.** If you lose these, it's like losing the key to your home for good—you won't be getting back in.

Different Ways to Invest

Investing in Bitcoin isn't just a one-size-fits-all approach. Here are a couple of strategies you might consider:

Long-Term Holding (HODLing): Many believe Bitcoin's price will continue to rise over the long haul. These folks buy Bitcoin and then hold onto it through ups and downs, like holding onto a bucking bull at the rodeo, wondering how you will finish.

It requires patience and a strong stomach, but it can be rewarding.

Trading: For those who prefer a bit more action, trading might be the way to go. This is like being on active duty, where you're always ready to jump into action. Day trading or swing trading involves buying and selling Bitcoin over shorter periods, aiming to profit from price fluctuations. It's more hands-on and requires a good understanding of market trends and technical trading skills. Not recommended for the beginner investor.

Common Mistakes to Avoid

Here's where a lot of newbies get burned. Avoid these pitfalls to keep your Bitcoin investment from going up in smoke:

Investing Blindly: Don't just buy Bitcoin because everyone says it's hot. Understand what you're getting into. Study up, stay informed, and make decisions based on knowledge, not hype.

Putting All Your Eggs in One Basket: Diversification is key in any good investment strategy. Don't pour all your money into Bitcoin. Spread it out across different assets to mitigate risk.

Falling for Scams: The Bitcoin world can be like a back alley at night—lots of shady characters. Watch out for too-good-to-be-true offers, phishing attempts, and fake websites.

Reacting to Volatility: Bitcoin's price can swing wildly. Don't panic and sell the moment things look bad, or buy in a frenzy when the price spikes. Like fighting a fire, stay calm, follow your plan, and keep your emotions in check.

That's your basic training on investing in Bitcoin, folks. Remember, every firefighter starts with the basics—hose management, ladder drills, and wearing the right gear. Investing in Bitcoin is no different. Start with the basics, stay safe, and keep learning. Onward to the next chapter, where we'll look at the future of Bitcoin. Get ready to climb higher!

Chapter 7:

Bitcoin ETFs – Investing in the Future

The Rise of Bitcoin ETFs

Let's kick the door down on a game-changer in the Bitcoin world: ETFs (Exchange-Traded Funds). Now, if you're picturing some Wall Street suits, you're spot on. But here's where it gets spicy: these ETFs are all about Bitcoin. They're a golden ticket for everyday investors to get a piece of the action without the headache of handling the actual coins. No wallets, no keys, just straight-up trading on the big board like you're buying stocks.

The first Bitcoin ETF to light up the board in the United States was the **ProShares Bitcoin Strategy ETF,** which hit the scene in October 2021. This was a big deal —not just a little spark but a full-on fireworks show.

It meant that Joe and Jane Doe could throw down on Bitcoin without having to dive into the digital trenches of actual Bitcoin ownership. But here's the twist—this bad boy deals in Bitcoin futures, not the coins themselves. It's a safer play, says the bigwigs, but it's a step removed from the real McCoy.

Then came the tag team of the **Valkyrie Bitcoin Strategy ETF** and the **VanEck Bitcoin Strategy ETF**, both also playing the futures game. They're like your backup hoses—there to make a splash without diving into the deep end.

But hold up, the plot thickens up in Canada, where the **Purpose Bitcoin ETF** kicked down the door as the first-ever ETF backed directly by Bitcoin—yeah, the real deal. When you throw cash at this, you're buying a slice of a fund that actually holds Bitcoin in its digital vault. This was a groundbreaking shift because it cut through the complexity and gave investors a straight shot at owning Bitcoin through a security.

Following Purpose, the Canadians rolled out the **Evolve Bitcoin ETF** and the **CI Galaxy Bitcoin ETF,** stashing actual Bitcoin and giving investors that direct exposure they crave, all wrapped up in the neat package of an ETF.

The Investment Company's Big Bet on Bitcoin ETFs

Now, imagine the biggest, baddest firefighter stepping into the ring, endorsing the most advanced fire-resistant suit out there. That's **BlackRock** diving into the Bitcoin ETF game with its iShares Bitcoin Trust. This isn't just any old player; this is the world's heavyweight champ of asset management swinging a 10 trillion dollar bat. Their move into Bitcoin ETFs? It's not just a nod of approval; it's a blazing siren to every investor out there that Bitcoin's ready for the big leagues and it's here to stay.

This isn't just about slapping a new paint job on their portfolio; it's BlackRock laying down the law, telling every big money outfit from here to Hong Kong that Bitcoin is where it's at. Think of it as the chief with the megaphone, rallying every firefighter in every firehouse across the globe. It's a game changer, making Bitcoin a bona fide part of the financial scene. As of August 2024 BlackRock holds close to 350,000 Bitcoins in their spot iShares Bitcoin Trust, which has amassed an estimated value of close to 21 billion dollars in only 8 months since launch!

With BlackRock's big boots on the ground, we're talking about kicking open doors to waves of investment, stabilizing Bitcoin's wild rides, and signaling to the powers-that-be (yeah, the regulators) that Bitcoin isn't just some back-alley dice game—it's mainstream.

And the ripple effect? It's like throwing a giant boulder into a pond. Expect a tidal wave of innovations, new strategies, investors, corporations and slick tools that make jumping into Bitcoin easy. This is big league stuff, folks!

Why Bitcoin ETFs Matter

Why all the noise about Bitcoin ETFs? Pull up a chair. These ETFs are like the new, turbo-charged fire trucks rolling into your station. They make jumping into Bitcoin investing as easy as buying a soda from the machine. No messing with digital wallets or fretting over private keys. Just pop your money in, and let the ETF handle the flames.

It's a win bigger than a five-alarm fire for Bitcoin, opening the floodgates for folks who might've been on the fence about diving into cryptocurrencies.

It's about bringing Bitcoin into the daylight, making it a staple in the financial diet of investors everywhere. So, strap in and hold on tight—investing in Bitcoin ETFs is like riding the ladder truck at full tilt. It's thrilling, it's smart, and it could change your financial future forever. Let's light this candle and see where it takes us!

--

As we wrap up our exploration of Bitcoin ETFs and how major players like BlackRock are bringing Bitcoin into the investment mainstream, let's pivot our attention to what lies ahead. Let's stoke the fires and peer into the future, where predictions, innovations, and potential hurdles paint a vivid landscape of possibilities for Bitcoin. Buckle up, because we're about to explore uncharted territories where the potential of Bitcoin stretches as far as the eye can see.

Chapter 8:

Blazing Ahead - The Future of Bitcoin

Strap on your helmets and crank up the engines, folks—
we're about to race into the roaring inferno that is the
future of Bitcoin. As we leave the realm of Bitcoin
ETFs in the dust, we're zooming into uncharted
territories packed with prophecies, power shifts, and
potential pitfalls. This isn't just a peek into what might
happen; it's a full-throttle dive into the what-ifs and
what-could-bes of Bitcoin. So, hold tight, because the
future is as unpredictable and exhilarating as a growing
wild fire!

What Experts Say

When it comes to predictions, experts are like a bunch of different bigwig business owners, market strategists, and or influencer with different weather reports—everyone's got an opinion on which way the wind's blowing and each one is correct in their own eyes. On one end, you've got the Bitcoin bulls, who are betting that Bitcoin's gonna soar sky-high, painting a future where Bitcoin isn't just a currency but a cornerstone of a new financial era.

They envision a world where Bitcoin is as everyday as your morning coffee, only much, much hotter.

Then there are the bears, armed with caution and a hefty dose of skepticism. They're eyeing the exits, warning us about everything from regulatory crackdowns to technological meltdowns. They see Bitcoin as a potential flashover that might just consume too much oxygen and fizzle out.

One thing is for certain if technology really melted down and the internet came to a screeching halt, everything would fall and today's generations don't have the tools to operate without that phone in their pocket!

Bitcoin's Role in the Economy

Let's sketch out Bitcoin's potential spot on the economic map. Imagine a world where Bitcoin shakes up the old financial regimes like a sledge hammer breaking through a wall. No more bank fees taking bites out of your budget, no more waiting days for a transaction to clear. Bitcoin could democratize dough, cutting out the middlemen and handing the power back to the people. It's about turning the financial system on its head, where access to money is as universal as air and water.

But let's not get too starry-eyed—this shake-up could kick up a storm. Traditional banks and financial bigwigs might not take kindly to this new kid on the block. The clash between the old guard and the new tech could be epic, reshaping or even ripping apart the financial fabric we've all been wrapped up in.

New Developments

On the tech front, Bitcoin never hits the brakes. Innovations like the **Lightning Network** are supercharging Bitcoin transactions, making them faster and cheaper—think of it as upgrading from an old fire truck to a jet-powered blaze battler. And with the rise of smart contracts and decentralized finance (DeFi), we're looking at a future where financial agreements are smart enough to execute themselves, minus the meddling middlemen that charge those pesky fees for just being there.

Could Bitcoin Fail?

Facing the flames, we've got to consider: Could Bitcoin crash and burn? Sure, as with any fire, there's always a risk it could get snuffed out. Technical glitches, a severe regulatory crackdown, or even a new, shinier crypto could douse Bitcoin's flames. And let's not forget, the crypto world is wild and unpredictable—today's treasure could easily become tomorrow's trash but this is our opportunity to create change by our involvement in its success.

How many large companies are closing their doors from department stores to restaurants because everything is going more digital or inflation has crushed their customer base? The answer is anything truly can fail and just like empires they rise and fall, but so do world reserve currencies. Just think about being a pioneer in Bitcoin seeing the future of financial freedom for the masses.

As we hose down the final embers, remember that forecasting Bitcoin's future is as tricky as predicting wildfire paths in a windstorm. It's thrilling, fraught with unknowns, yet packed with potential. So keep your gear at the ready and your mind open because the Bitcoin adventure is far from over. Next up, we'll keep the adrenaline pumping as we explore a few more fiery frontiers.

Chapter 9:

Riding the Bitcoin Wave - Staying Informed and Involved

Gear up, crew! As we blast out of the fiery future of Bitcoin, let's not leave you hanging like a lone firefighter without backup. Staying sharp in the Bitcoin world isn't just about knowing your stuff—it's about being plugged into the pulse of the Bitcoin community. This chapter is your go-to guide for keeping your knowledge hot and your actions cool in the sizzling world of Bitcoin. Let's roll!

Keeping Up with Bitcoin

Keeping track of Bitcoin is like trying to stay ahead of a wildfire—things move fast, and if you blink, you might miss a shift in the wind. To keep your head in the game, you need reliable sources. Here's your fire chief's list of must-follows:

Crypto News Sites: Stick to the heavyweights like **CoinDesk**, **CoinTelegraph**, and **CryptoSlate**. They're the dispatchers of the crypto world, sending out updates, breaking news, and in-depth analysis.

Social Media and Forums: Twitter now known as **X** is the loudspeaker of crypto chatter, where influencers, traders, and developers shoot the breeze. **Reddit**'s r/Bitcoin and r/CryptoCurrency are like the bustling firehouse kitchens where everyone gathers to swap stories, strategies and solve the world's problems.

Podcasts: Tune into podcasts like **"The Pomp Podcast"** while you're dousing flames or hitting the gym. They bring experts right into your ears, discussing everything from Bitcoin basics to the latest blockchain innovations.

Joining the Community

Bitcoin isn't just a currency; it's a community. Whether you're a rookie or a seasoned Bitcoiner, connecting with fellow Bitcoin buffs can keep your enthusiasm burning bright. It's where you can go to connect with like minded people who aren't just sheepishly making their way through life.

They are leaders who want more from life and want you to be a part of that growth.

Meetups and Conferences: Check out Eventbrite for crypto gatherings. Conferences like **Bitcoin 2025** taking place in Las Vegas that attract enthusiasts from around the globe and are packed with workshops, talks, new developments and networking events.

Online Communities: Dive into forums and social media groups. Places like **BitcoinTalk Forum** and **the Bitcoin Community** on **Discord** are buzzing hives of activity where you can ask questions, get advice, and share your experiences.

Local Bitcoin Clubs: Some cities have their own Bitcoin clubs, perfect for meeting like-minded folks. It's like joining a volunteer fire brigade but for slinging crypto knowledge instead of hoses.

Being a Responsible Bitcoin Owner

Owning Bitcoin is a big responsibility—think of it as handling dangerous equipment that can either save lives or cause chaos. Here's how to wield your tools wisely:

Educate Yourself: Keep your skills sharp. The more you know, the safer you'll be. Stay updated on security practices, legal changes, and market trends.

Secure Your Assets: Use strong, unique passwords for your wallets and exchanges. Consider a hardware wallet for an extra layer of security—it's like having a fireproof safe.

Backup Everything: Regularly backup your wallet data. Store your backup and recovery phrases in a secure location—losing these is like forgetting where you parked the car.

Final Thoughts

As we cool down the engines and roll back into the station, remember, the journey into Bitcoin is ongoing. The landscape is always changing, with new challenges and opportunities at every turn. Whether you're just starting out or you're a seasoned bitcoiner, stay curious, stay connected, and keep learning.

Don't just watch from the sidelines; get involved, ask questions, and dive into discussions. Bitcoin isn't just about making a quick buck—it's about being part of a community that's at the forefront of a financial revolution. So, grab your gear, team up with your fellow crypto enthusiasts, and keep pushing the boundaries. Who knows what treasures you'll find or the fires you'll extinguish along the way.

With that, our Bitcoin guidebook comes to a close but your adventure is just getting started. Stay fiery, stay fearless, and let's make some waves in the world of Bitcoin.

Acknowledgments

This journey through "Bitcoin for the Working Class: A Blue-Collar Guide to Financial Freedom" would not have been possible without the support and inspiration from many incredible individuals.

First, a heartfelt thank you to the hardworking men and women who embody the spirit of this book—your resilience fuels these pages. I am grateful to the Bitcoin enthusiasts and experts whose insights have profoundly shaped this guide.

Special appreciation goes to my fellow firefighters for their support as I navigated the complex world of Bitcoin and to many discussions around the kitchen table, and to my editor, whose expertise transformed my initial drafts into the polished work you read today.

Acknowledgements

To my family, thank you for your endless patience and encouragement. Your support has been my foundation throughout this process, and I am thankful you have taken the leap into Bitcoin as well.

And to you, the reader, thank you for embarking on this journey with me. I hope this book empowers you as much as writing it has empowered me.

With deepest gratitude,

Captain Matt Jackson

Meet the Captain

Alright, folks, strap in and get ready. You're about to meet a man who's not just fighting fires—he's living the American Dream, one blaze at a time. Meet Captain Matt Jackson, the no-nonsense Captain in Las Vegas, NV. This guy's the kind of leader who makes you want to grab a shovel and dig in right alongside him, even if you're just hearing his story from the sidelines.

Captain Jackson isn't just a firefighter. He's a patriot with a heart as big as his boots. His loyalty to his country is as fierce as his commitment to putting out fires and saving lives. From a young age he always strived to be a man of integrity and commitment climbing all the way to the rank of Eagle Scout by the time he was 16 years old. But his drive to success didn't stop there, he then went and got his degree in paramedicine and fire science.

Working in the family business growing up he loved the growth of entrepreneurship and started a successful entertainment and event company, with his Fiancé, in Las Vegas while working in the fire service.

He's got the American flag flying high and a family that he'd do anything for. His home is a shrine to hard work, faith, and the American spirit, and he's got a no BS approach to life that's as refreshing as a cold drink on a hot day.

Captain Jackson's passion for learning and a drive to get ahead goes beyond the call of duty. Amid the chaos of his 48 hour (sometimes 72 hour) shifts, he made time to educate himself about Bitcoin—a modern frontier in the financial world. With the same determination he uses to battle blazes, he dived head first into the world of digital currency. He poured over books, scoured online resources, and is even attending seminars to get a handle on this new financial beast.

This book isn't just about the grind of the daily shift; it's about making every moment, and every paycheck count. Captain Jackson's mission is simple: to show every blue-collar worker out there that the American Dream is within reach, and it's not just about working hard—it's about smartly investing in your future.

He's the guy who believes that with sweat on your brow, grit in your gut, and a bit of savvy financial know-how, you can take life by the horns and wrestle it to the ground.

Captain Jackson's not here to sugarcoat things. He's here to tell it straight and has got a message for those who roll up their sleeves and punch the clock every day.

"You're the backbone of this country, and you deserve to get every ounce of success you've earned, plus a little extra for your smarts."

So get ready. Captain Jackson is about to take you on a ride through the real deal of blue-collar life, where hard work, loyalty, and freedom aren't just ideals—they're the way you live and breathe. If you're ready to get the most out of every day and every dollar, and maybe even dip your toes into the world of Bitcoin, you're in the right place.

Made in the USA
Columbia, SC
27 November 2024

47678776R00046